WELCOME TO ROSSLYN Chapel, which has been in the ownership of my family since its foundation in 1446 and which is still used today as a place of worship. I hope that this book will help you to enjoy the rich complexity of its history and architecture.

In 1996, we established the Rosslyn Chapel Trust, a registered charity, to oversee the continuing programme of conservation. By visiting Rosslyn, you are helping us to care for this most remarkable medieval buildin~

Rosslyn.

CHAPTER I

ROSSLYN: A SHORT HISTORY

ROSSLYN CHAPEL, OR the Collegiate Chapel of St Matthew as it was to have been, was founded in 1446 by Sir William St Clair, third and last St Clair Prince of Orkney. It is in fact only part of what was intended to be a larger cruciform building with a tower at its centre. Though incomplete, it took 40 years to build.

More than thirty-seven such collegiate churches were built in Scotland between the reigns of James I and James IV (1406–1513). They were secular foundations intended to spread intellectual and spiritual knowledge, and the extravagance of their construction depended on the wealth of their founder.

After Sir William died in 1484, he was buried in the unfinished Chapel and the larger building he had planned was never realised. But the foundations of the nave are said to have been excavated in the nineteenth century and found to extend ninety-one feet beyond the Chapel's original west door, under the existing baptistery and churchyard.

What was built, however, is extraordinary enough.

'This building, I believe, may be pronounced unique, and I am confident it will be found curious, elaborate and singularly interesting, impossible to designate by any given or familiar term,' wrote Britton in his *Architectural Antiquities of Britain* (1812), adding somewhat despairingly that its 'variety and eccentricity are not to be defined by any words of common acceptation'.

The principal authority on the history of the Chapel and the St Clair family is Father Richard Augustine Hay, Canon of St Genevieve in Paris and Prior of St Piermont. He examined historical records and charters of the St Clairs and completed a three-volume study in 1700, parts of which were published in 1835 as *A Genealogie of the Sainteclaires of Rosslyn*. His research was timely, since the original documents subsequently disappeared.

The history of the St Clair family is described in Chapter Four, but of the founder Father Hay said this:

'Prince William, his age creeping on him, came to consider how he had spent his times past, and how he was to spend his remaining days. Therefore, to the end, that he might not seem altogether unthankful to God for the benefices he received from Him, it came into his mind to build a house for God's service, of most curious work, the which that it might be done with greater glory and splendour he caused artificers to be brought from other regions and foreign kingdoms and caused daily to be abundance of all kinds of workmen present as masons, carpenters, smiths,

barrowmen and quarriers . . . the foundation of this work he caused to be laid in the year of our Lord 1446, and to the end, the work might be more rare, first he caused draughts [plans] to be drawn upon eastland boards [imported Baltic timber], and he made the carpenters carve them according to the draughts thereon, and he gave them for patterns to the masons, that they might cut the like in stone and because he thought the masons had not a convenient place to lodge in . . . he made them build the town of Rosline that now is extant and gave everyone a house and lands. He rewarded the masons according to their degree, as to the Master Mason, he gave £40 yearly, and to everyone of the rest, £10. . . .'

Rosslyn Chapel from the air

Sir William's son and successor to the barony of Rosslyn, Sir Oliver St Clair, roofed the choir with its stone vault but did no more to fulfil his father's original design.

The Chapel was generously endowed by the founder, with provision for a provost, six prebendaries, and two choristers, and in 1523 by his grandson, also Sir William, with land for dwelling houses and gardens. On February 26th, 1571, however, just forty-eight years after this last endowment, there is a record of the provost and prebendaries resigning because of the endowments being taken 'by force and violence' into secular hands as the influence of the Reformation took hold.

The Presbytery records of Dalkeith reveal that in 1589 William Knox, brother of John Knox and minister of Cockpen, was censured 'for baptizing the Laird of Rosling's bairne' in Rosslyn

Samuel Dukinfield Swarbreck,
*Rosslyn Chapel: the East
Aisle*, plate XIII from
Sketches in Scotland.
Tinted lithograph, 1837

Chapel, which was described as a 'house and monument of idolatrie, and not ane place appointit for teiching the word and ministratioun of ye sacramentis'.

The following year, the Presbytery forbade Mr George Ramsay, minister of Lasswade, from burying the wife of a later Oliver St Clair in the Chapel. The St Clairs had not yet succumbed to the Reformation and remained Roman Catholics.

This Oliver St Clair was repeatedly warned to destroy the altars in the Chapel and in 1592 was summoned to appear before the General Assembly and threatened with excommunication if the altars remained standing after August 17th, 1592. On August 31st, the same George Ramsay reported that 'the altars of Roslene were haille demolishit'. From that time the Chapel ceased to be used as a house of prayer and soon fell into disrepair.

In 1650, during the Civil War, Cromwell's troops under General Monk attacked the Castle and his horses were stabled in the Chapel.

On December 11th, 1688, shortly after the Protestant William of Orange landed in England and displaced the Catholic James II, a mob from Edinburgh and some villagers from Roslin entered and damaged the Chapel. Their object was to destroy furniture and vestments, which were now regarded as Popish and idolatrous.

The Chapel remained abandoned until 1736, when James St Clair glazed the windows for the first time, repaired the roof, and relaid the floor with flagstones. The boundary wall was also built at this time.

When Dorothy Wordsworth visited the Chapel on September 17th, 1807, she remarked: 'Went to view the inside of the Chapel of Roslyn, which is kept locked up, and so preserved from the injuries it might otherwise receive from idle boys, but as nothing is done to keep it together, it must, in the end, fall. The architecture within is exquisitely beautiful.'

Further repairs to the Chapel were undertaken at the beginning of the nineteenth century and in 1861 it was agreed by James Alexander, 3rd Earl of Rosslyn, that Sunday services should begin again. He instructed the Edinburgh architect David Bryce to carry out restoration work. The carvings in the Lady Chapel were attended to and stones were relaid in the sacristy and an altar established there. The Chapel was rededicated on Tuesday, April 22nd, 1862, by the Bishop of Edinburgh; the Bishop of Brechin preached from the text, 'Lord, I have loved the habitation of thy house, and the place where thine honour dwelleth' (Psalms 26: 8).

The Reverend R. Cole, then resident military chaplain at Greenlaw Barracks near Penicuick, became private chaplain to the Earl. Lady Helen Wedderburn, daughter of the 3rd Earl of Airlie, who lived nearby at Rosebank, organised a subscription from which some of the interior fittings were provided.

John Slezer, *The Chappell of Rosslin*, from *Theatrum Scotiae*. Engraving, 1693

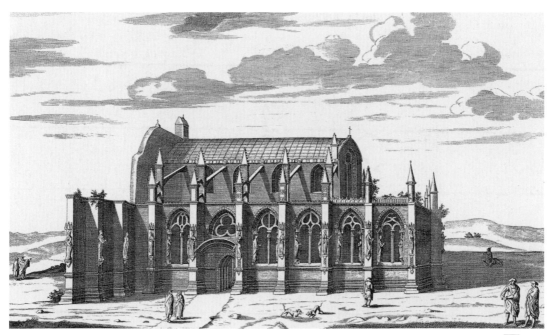

In 1880–1, Francis Robert, 4th Earl of Rosslyn, added the apse to serve as a baptistery with an organ loft above. The work is by Andrew Kerr. The Earl also filled the baptistery arch with the handsome oak tracery which you see today, decorated with his crest. Together with the two Chapel doors, this is the only wood used in the construction of the building.

The cost of the work was £758.8.6, with a further £34.18.0 to Andrew Kerr for fees, design work, and superintendence. Kerr told the Earl that a party of visitors 'had remarked that it was wonderful that such young men could be entrusted to execute such carving', to which the estate factor 'very coolly replied, that it was not wonderful here, as the finest pillar in the Chapel was the work of an apprentice boy.'

The Earl was happy with the work and in a letter to Kerr on November 16th, 1880, wrote: 'I must say that the author pronounces your building a complete success.'

In 1915, a report on the fabric by architect Sir Robert Lorimer observed: 'The stone work of the Chapel is in fairly good order and requires very little to be done to it . . . a few of the stones are crumbling but not to an extent to cause any alarm. The condition of the roof is not satisfactory . . . and there are a number of gaps and cracks all over.' His advice that the exterior of the roof be covered with asphalt was followed.

In 1942 the Chapel was almost closed for a second time when a constituency official wrote to the Minister of Labour, Ernest Bevin MP, 'that the Episcopalian Church at Roslin was almost empty every Sunday . . . on a recent Sunday there was a congregation of only two, and that apart from the Clergyman's labour there must be other workers employed in cleaning and looking after the church and I suggest that steps are taken to close it down.'

A copy of the letter was sent to Gwilym Lloyd George MP, the Minister of Fuel, who in turn wrote to the Secretary of State for Scotland in the following terms:

'I enclose a copy of a letter from David Robertson which causes me considerable embarrassment, who am I, a Welshman, that I should do anything that might imperil the eternal salvation of one Scottish Episcopalian. In any case, from the fuel point of view, I doubt whether I would be justified in securing a small economy of fuel in this world at the possible cost of a disproportionate expenditure of it on myself in the next.'

The Chapel remained open.

Further work was carried out by my father in the 1950's when the sacristy roof was repaired and the interior carvings cleaned by hand over a period of several years. He also added the stained glass windows in the baptistery.

A report of May 1954 from the Ancient Monuments Branch of the Ministry of Works records that 'surfaces covered with green algae will be scrubbed down with stiff bristle brushes . . . using a solution of .880 ammonia and water. Water will then be used copiously until the surfaces are clean and free from dirt and

vegetation. Flaky patches will be sealed off . . . Hollow areas in ornament will receive special treatment by grouting . . . and when the surfaces are thoroughly dry they will be hardened with silica fluoride of magnesium at a rate of 1lb per two gallons of water.'

Rosslyn Chapel with the Pentland Hills

This work was in accordance with the thinking of the time but not, unfortunately, with current conservation philosophy. The effect of the magnesium fluoride – a cementitious slurry – was to seal the surface of the masonry with an impermeable coating, so that the stone became saturated with water containing soluble pollutants. In addition, the coldness of the wet stone encouraged condensation. A 1995 report confirmed that damage was occurring and that humidity in the Chapel was very high. It recommended that steps should be taken to dry out the saturated masonry, remove if possible the cementitious coating, and restore the permeability of the richly carved interior surfaces of the Chapel.

In March 1997, a free-standing steel structure was erected to cover the Chapel. It will enable the stone fabric of the roof vaults to dry outwards, away from the carved interior surfaces. In due course the bituminous felt, asphalt, and concrete coverings of the stone roof vaults will be removed to assist this process. Stone and mortar repairs to the external walls, pinnacles, and buttresses, renewal of the rainwater disposal arrangements, repairs to the stained glass, and appropriate repair and conservation of the interior are all required. The coverings over the stone vaulted roofs will be renewed in lead and ways of removing the cementitious slurry are being investigated, in order that this magnificent building can be preserved for future generations to use and admire.

All this work is being overseen by our architect James Simpson, who has loved and cared for both Chapel and Castle over many years, and whose loyal support it is a pleasure to acknowledge here.

CHAPTER II

A Tour of Rosslyn Chapel

T HIS SECTION OF the book is intended as a guide as you look around the Chapel and I hope it will help you to find and interpret some of its most significant features. Some of the carvings are difficult to locate and for that reason the style of this chapter may seem a little authoritarian. Please feel free to follow the suggested route or to devise one of your own.

You will be approaching the Chapel from the north.

Pause for a moment halfway along the pathway leading to the north door and look up above the three large clerestory windows in front of you. You will notice at the edge of the roof a series of shields. Although difficult to distinguish clearly, you may just be able to make out, on alternate shields, the following inscription,

W   L   S   F   Y   C   Y   Z   O   G   M iii 1 L

which translates as

William Lord Sinclair Fundit Yis College Ye Zeir Of God MCCCCL (1450)

This suggests either that Father Hay's foundation date of 1446 is inaccurate or perhaps that the foundations themselves took 4 years to complete.

On either side of the north door, two water spouts in the form of gargoyles peer down menacingly, although one respected architectural historian describes them as 'jolly'. In the window to the right of the door, in its bottom right corner, you will see a soldier on horseback. In the bottom left corner are two rams locking horns. Between this window and the north door, under the gargoyle, is a hunched figure with a stick pressed behind its bent knees. It is echoed by a similar figure on the buttress directly to your right.

In the window to the left of the door is a fox making off with a goose, with the farmer, or perhaps his more agile wife, in pursuit. In the opposite corner of this window is a cherub playing a musical instrument. You will find more of this angelic orchestra inside.

There will be an opportunity for a more detailed look at the exterior of the building in due course, but let us now enter the Chapel by the north door.

Opposite page. The choir

THE CHOIR

HAVING ENTERED THE Chapel, sit for a moment in the centre of the building, looking towards the main altar. You are now facing east. Above, the barrel-vaulted roof is divided into five compartments of different design separated by elaborately carved stone bands known as ribs. From east to west (front to back) the compartments contain:

1. Daisies
2. Lilies
3. Flowers
4. Roses
5. Stars

On the second rib from the east, towards the centre of the Chapel roof, you may just be able to distinguish a pendant keystone with a pair of hands holding a shield on which is carved the Sinclair engrailed cross.

The part of the building in which you are now sitting, the choir, is forty-eight feet long, eighteen feet wide, and forty-four feet in height. It stands between thirteen pillars, which together form an arcade of twelve pointed arches, five arches on each side and two behind the main altar. Over this series of arches is a continuous line of carved decoration known as an ornamental string course. Above this, on each side of the choir, are five clerestory windows with single lights. Above the altar is the large east window, which has two lights.

Between each of the side windows you will notice two brackets, one above the other. There are twelve on each side, all of which contained statues destroyed in the sixteenth century at the time of the Reformation. The statue of the Virgin Mary holding the infant Jesus, on the bracket directly above the main altar, is a Victorian addition.

Opposite page. The roof

Left. Pendant keystone with Sinclair engrailed cross

The stained glass windows above the altar depict the resurrection. In the left-hand window are three women arriving at the sepulchre; in the right-hand window two angels sit, one holding a scroll on which is written 'He is not here but is risen'. An inscription which is not visible reads:

'To the glory of God: in most affectionate remembrance of his only sister Harriet Elizabeth St Clair, daughter of James Alexander, third Earl of Rosslyn, and wife of George Herbert, Count Munster of Derneburg in Hanover, this window was entirely restored and filled with stained glass, November 1896 by Francis Robert, fourth Earl of Rosslyn. She was born June 26 1831; married August 22 1865; and died at Derneburg, November 29 1867, where, by her own request, she was buried.'

Whatever stained glass existed in the Chapel before the nineteenth century was destroyed during the Reformation and for many years the only protection from the elements was in the form of shutters on the outside of the windows, where their iron hinge pins are still visible. The shutters were removed when the windows were glazed with clear glass in 1736.

Now turn to your right and walk towards the south door, opposite where you entered, stopping before you come to the pillars that separate the choir from the south aisle. If you look up at the top of the pillar to your right, you can just make out a lion

Arch with carvings of
the apostles and martyrs

and a horse, or possibly a unicorn – although, if it is the latter, its horn is missing. The lion is often associated with the resurrection of Christ and the unicorn is symbolic of his incarnation. The animals appear to be fighting, the unicorn with a ring and chain placed loosely round its neck.

On the arch linking this pillar with the pillar to its right, starting immediately above the unicorn's head, are sixteen figures representing the twelve apostles and four martyrs, each with a halo and most bearing the instruments of their martyrdom. The writers of the scriptures appear to have books in their hands.

Now go to the rear of the choir, near the entrance to the baptistery, and look up again at the last compartment of the roof. Among its stars are to be found four angels, the moon, the sun, a dove, and, barely visible in the bottom right hand corner of the north side, the face of Christ with his hand raised in blessing.

THE NORTH AISLE

W E NOW LEAVE the choir for the north aisle, starting at the north-west corner of the Chapel, to the right of the baptistery. Here you will see a monument to George, 4th Earl of Caithness and great grandson of the founder. The memorial is surmounted by an artichoke and bears the Caithness coat of arms and family motto, 'Commit thy verk to God'.

To the right of the tomb, lying against the north wall, is the burial stone of the William St Clair who died fighting the Moors in Spain in 1330 (see page 42 in Chapter Four and photo on page 55). On the surface of the stone is the carved outline of a sword of the 'West Highland' type. Alongside it, the central motif is a floriated cross (at left) forming a chalice or grail on a long stem and a calvary base. The floriated cross is often associated with the Knights Templar, whose connection with Rosslyn is discussed in Chapter Five. On the side nearest to you is the name Willhm de Sinncler. At the right-hand end of the stone are the letters ER, one below the other. They may stand for *Et Reliqua*, meaning 'and the remains' or 'and relics'.

This stone originally lay at the site of an earlier church, which stood below and to the south-west of the present Chapel in what is now the village graveyard. The size of the stone, thirty-nine by eleven inches, suggests that it was intended as a tomb marker rather than an exterior grave slab, for which it would be too small.

On the west wall to the left of the Caithness tomb you will see

Opposite page. The north aisle

Right. The Caithness tomb

Above. Two dragons and angel holding a scroll

Below left. Devil with kneeling couple
Below right. Angel holding a cross

a pillar, at the top of which is a carving of two dragons intertwined and underneath an angel holding a scroll and looking towards the north door. There are many other examples in the Chapel of angels bearing scrolls or open books, suggesting a theme from the Book of Revelations: 'I could see the dead, great and small, standing before the throne: and books were opened. Then another book was opened, the roll of the living. From what was written in these books the dead were judged upon the record of their deeds.' (Revelations 20: 12.)

Now stand with your back to the Caithness tomb and at the top of the pillar in front of you to the right, facing the dragons, is a figure said to represent the prodigal son feeding the swine. On the opposite side of this pillar is one bird feeding another.

In the first window on your left are two important carvings. At the base of the window, on the left-hand side, the devil scowls in anger and disappointment as the kneeling couple beside him gaze at the right-hand corner of the window, where an angel is holding a cross.

Further along the aisle on your left is the north door through which you entered. It is known as the Bachelor's Door, reflecting the segregation of the sexes which required ladies to enter the Chapel from the south and men from the north.

To the right of the door is a small wall pillar rising up from the stone ledge and at its very top is a plaited crown of thorns. The ledge may in fact be a bench and it has been suggested that the expression 'the weak to the wall' originated from the practice of providing such seating for those unable to stand.

To the left of the door is another small wall pillar and above it

Far left. The crown of thorns

Left. The crucifixion

is a representation of the crucifixion. You will notice that the cross of Jesus is surrounded by nine figures and that at the rear, to the saviour's right, is a ladder. This suggests that the carving may represent, in particular, the descent from the cross.

Turn with your back to the north door and look at the pillars directly to your left and right. At the top of the pillar to your left, facing the crown of thorns which you have just seen, is a carving of angels rolling away the stone from Christ's tomb. On the pillar to your right a group of three figures, one without a head, is observing the crucifixion scene on the wall opposite. Their identity is open to debate. They could be Mary Magdalene, Mary the mother of James and Joseph, and Salome, wife of Zebedee (St Mark 15: 40) – but one figure appears to be a man. Or they could be Mary Magdalene, Simon Peter, and another disciple (St John 20: 1–3). A third interpretation is that the group symbolises the three divisions of the human family who took part in and witnessed the crucifixion:

'And Pilate wrote a title, and put it on the cross. And the writing was, JESUS OF NAZARETH THE KING OF THE JEWS . . . and it was written in *Hebrew*, and *Greek*, and *Latin*.' (St John 19: 19–20.)

Below left. Angels rolling away the stone from Christ's tomb

Below right. Three figures observing the crucifixion

If you now walk east along the north aisle, you will see another wall pillar to your left, between the first and second windows. At its top is an angel holding a seal depicting the lamb of God, an emblem said to be associated with the Knights Templar.

Turn around and face the pillar behind you. At its top, opposite the lamb of God, is an enormous lion's head with a pair of hands forcing open its jaws. The head and eyes of the lion are facing towards the north door of the Chapel and are clearly distinguishable. The hands are probably Samson's: 'And behold, a young lion roared against him. And the Spirit of the Lord came mightily upon him, and he rent him as he would have rent a kid, and he had nothing in his hand.' (Judges 14: 5–6.) To the right of this carving, facing west at the same level, is a plaited crown. To the left, facing east, is an elephant.

Turn around and look at the window to your right. At the bottom of the window, on the left-hand side, is an angel holding a shield with an engrailed cross. The engrailed cross is the coat of arms of the Sinclair family and also forms part of the coat of arms of the earls of Rosslyn. As you will see, it is repeated throughout the building – on the front of the altars of the Lady Chapel, on the Caithness tomb, and on the roof of the sacristy.

Top. Agnus Dei, the lamb of God

Above. Lion's head, at top left of the picture, and plaited crown, at top right

Right. Angel with engrailed cross

Architrave with carvings of the
Lord and seven bishops or
kings

Now turn and face the main altar. Between the pillars to your
left and right you will notice an incised slab on the floor and on it
the carved image of a knight in armour. The knight's hands are
uplifted and joined as if in prayer. On each side of his head is a
small shield with a lion rampant and at his feet lies a greyhound,
although the latter is almost indistinguishable.

This is believed by some to be the burial place of William
St Clair, founder of the Chapel. However, the heraldry appears to
have no connection with the St Clairs and it seems more probable
that it is the burial place of Alexander Sutherland of Dunbeath,
father of the founder's second wife, who in his will dated
November 15th, 1456, expressed a particular wish for 'my body to
be gravyt in the Colledge Kirk of ane hie and mightie Lord
William, Earl of Caithnes and Orknay, Lord Sinclare &c, in
Rosling, ner quhair himself thinks to ly, where the said Lord Erle
thinks speedfull.'

Another possibility is that it is the tombstone of the Sir William
St Clair who died while escorting the heart of Robert Bruce to the
Holy Land in 1330. If so, the animals to left and right of his head
are not lions but his two hounds, Help and Hold, and the animal
beneath his feet is a stag. The significance of these creatures, if
such they be, is explained on page 42 in Chapter Four.

Walk a few steps further along the aisle, beyond the pillar to
the left of this tombstone, and then turn right around to face west.
Above you, connecting the pillar to the north wall, is an architrave
with eight figures. The central figure is sitting upright with his
hands raised while the seven others, with crowns on their heads
and one with a harp, are lying horizontally.

One interpretation of this scene is that it represents our Lord,
seated in glory, addressing the bishops of the seven churches in
Asia: 'I am the Alpha and the Omega, the first and the last: and,
what thou seest, write in a book, and send it unto the seven
churches which are in Asia.' (Revelations 2: 11). Or it may be a
reference to Psalm 72, verse 11: 'Yea, all kings shall fall down
before him: all nations shall serve him.'

Turn right around again and in front of you, a step up from the
level of the choir, is the Lady Chapel.

THE LADY CHAPEL & SACRISTY

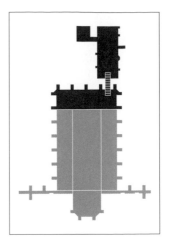

THE LADY CHAPEL is fifteen feet high, seven and a half feet deep, and extends to the whole thirty-five foot width of the Chapel. As you enter, you will notice that there are four altars in front of you and to your right. They were dedicated on February 5th, 1523, from left to right, to St Matthew, the Blessed Virgin, St Andrew, and St Peter. This last altar is above the stairs which lead to the sacristy and is often referred to as the 'high altar'.

The brass plaques just under the windows in front of you read: 'In memory of dear parents by whom this chapel was restored to the service of God A.D. 1862, Ac majorem dei gloriam [to the greater glory of God] the stained glass windows in the Ladye Chapel were placed by Francis Robert, fourth Earl of Rosslyn, A.D. 1867.'

The six double windows, one at each end of the Lady Chapel and one above each of the four altars, are the work of Clayton and Bell of London and show the twelve apostles. From left to right they are:
1. St Peter and St James the Greater
2. St John and St Andrew
3. St Philip and St Bartholomew
4. St Matthew and St Thomas
5. St James the Less and St Thaddeus
6. St Simon and St Matthias

Now stand between the altars to St Matthew and the Blessed Virgin (the first and second from the left), and face south towards the stairs to the sacristy. You will see above you, hanging from the roof directly over the brass floor plaque to the memory of Harriet Elizabeth, Countess of Rosslyn, a pendant boss with an eight-pointed star on its lower surface. This represents the star of Bethlehem and around the sides of the star you will see eight figures associated with the story of the birth of Christ.

Walk round to its other side and on its south point you can see the virgin and child; to the left, the manger; on the west, north-west, and north points, the three wise men, each holding a staff; then the angel of death; then other figures associated with the nativity.

At the very top of the three pillars separating the Lady Chapel from the choir are angels singing and playing instruments, including the bagpipes, in celebration. They represent the 'heavenly host praising God' referred to in St Luke 2: 13.

The Chapel is rich in carvings of the 'green man'. Over one hundred have been counted in the interior of the building, a profusion of pagan fertility symbols not unexpected in a place so influenced by the Celtic tradition. One of the finest examples is in the Lady Chapel. Stand between the altars to the Blessed Virgin and St Andrew (the second and third from the left), facing east. The carving is above and in front of you on the end of a boss. If you stand directly under it, you will see the green man full face.

Opposite page. The Lady Chapel

Below. Engraving of pendant boss showing figures associated with the birth of Christ

Angel playing the bagpipes

The green man symbolised the capacity for great goodness and the parallel scope for significant evil. The story of Robin Hood has its origins in this legend and was a popular maytide play in Scotland during the fifteenth and sixteenth centuries, often performed by gypsies.

The St Clair family in general and in particular Sir William St Clair, great grandson of the founder of the Chapel, were known to be sympathetic to the plight of the gypsies in an age when the laws of the country persecuted them severely.

In 1599, while Lord Justice General, this Sir William 'delivered ane Egyptian from the gibbet in the Burrow Moore, ready to be strangled; upon which accoumpt the whole body of gypsies were, of old, accustomed to gather in the Stanks of Rosslyn every year, where they acted severall plays, during the month of May and June. There are two towers which were allowed for their residence, the one called Robin Hood and the other Little John.'

The heads of the St Clair family were hereditary Grand Master Masons of Scotland, as described in Chapter Four, and throughout the Lady Chapel you will see figures of angels whose distinctive positions are significant in the rites of freemasonry. Just to the left of the altar to the Blessed Virgin, at head height, is a carving of particular importance. It shows Lucifer, the fallen angel, bound and upside down.

This stone forms the base of a statue niche. If you stand on the other (south) side of the altar to the Blessed Virgin and look up to the top of this statue niche, you will see to its left, beneath an angel holding a scroll, what is said to be a carving of the death mask of Robert Bruce.

Now stand between the altars to St Matthew and the Blessed Virgin (the first and second from the left) and face north. In the corner some six feet above the altar to St Matthew is a carved head with an angel to the left of it. A matching head can be seen in the south–west corner above the high altar. On the ribbed arch rising immediately to the left of the angel is a series of figures, sixteen in all, going up the face of one rib and down the rib opposite. Each of these figures has a skeleton next to it and this illustration is commonly known as the 'dance of death' or 'danse macabre', an allegorical representation of death's supremacy over

Lucifer, the fallen angel

Green man

Above left. The dance of death, with detail (*above right*)

Opposite page. The Mason's Pillar

mankind. From the right we have:

1. An abbot
2. An abbess
3. (Indistinguishable)
4. A lady looking in a mirror

5. (Indistinguishable)
6. A bishop
7. A cardinal
8. A courtier

Going down the other side we have:

9. A king
10. A farmer
11. A husband and wife
12. A child

13. A sportsman
14. A gardener and his spade
15. A carpenter
16. A ploughman

The dance of death was frequently represented in pictures and in drama. It was a theme much interpreted by Hans Holbein the Younger (1497–1543). It is found on the walls of Dominican cemeteries in Switzerland and in frescoes at the Tower of London. There is a particularly fine example in the Cimetière des Innocents in Paris, completed in 1424. But Rosslyn's is generally believed to be one of the earliest, if not the first, to be carved in stone.

There are many other extraordinary carvings in the Lady Chapel and you may wish to spend a few minutes exploring them.

On leaving the Lady Chapel, turn left towards the stairs to the sacristy and stop in front of the first pillar on your left. This is the Mason's Pillar, said to be the work of the master mason. Although splendid, it is altogether less elaborate in design and execution than the work of his apprentice, which we shall see in a moment. If you now stand between the Mason's Pillar and the plain pillar to its right and look up at the top of the Mason's Pillar, you will see

above the capital, facing south, a figure of an angel holding a bible and proclaiming the gospel or good news of Jesus' birth.

Walk on behind the main altar towards the south wall and on your left, at the top of the stairs to the sacristy, stands the Apprentice Pillar. Like others in the Chapel it stands eight feet in height, but it is quite different in the delicacy and sophistication of its carving. In 'An Account of the Chapel of Rosslyn', written in 1774, Dr Forbes, Bishop of Caithness, describes the legend in these words:

'The Master Mason, having received from the Founder the model of a pillar of exquisite workmanship and design, hesitated to carry it out until he had been to Rome or some other foreign part and seen the original. He went abroad and in his absence an apprentice, having dreamt that he had finished the pillar, at once set to work and carried out the design as it now stands, a perfect marvel of workmanship. The Master Mason on his return, seeing the pillar completed, instead of being delighted at the success of his pupil, was so stung with envy that he asked who had dared to do it in his absence. On being told that it was his apprentice, he was so inflamed with rage and passion that he struck him with his mallet, killed him on the spot and paid the penalty for his rash and cruel act.'

The participants in this story are represented in carvings elsewhere in the Chapel (see page 32).

At the top of the Apprentice Pillar, overlooking the stairs to the sacristy and facing the south wall, is a representation of Isaac lying bound upon the altar. Adjacent is a ram caught in a thicket by his horns. Dr Forbes, in his account of the Chapel, refers to a figure of Abraham with hands lifted in prayer, but this has been destroyed.

Near the bottom of the pillar, by the stairs to the sacristy, is a Stafford Knot. This emblem, like a figure of eight, is associated with the English patriot Hereward the Wake, who opposed William the Conqueror and whose descendants, the Dukes of Buckingham, adopted the symbol as their family badge.

At the base of the Apprentice Pillar you will find eight dragons and from their mouths emerges the vine which winds itself around the pillar. There may be a link here to Scandinavian mythology, in which the eight dragons of Neifelheim were said to lie at the base of Yggdrasil, the great ash tree which bound together heaven, earth, and hell. The founder's connection with Orkney perhaps provided the inspiration for this symbolism.

Now we can descend the stairs to the sacristy.

This part of the building may be older than the Chapel itself. One reason for believing this is that the seventeenth century engineer and topographical draughtsman John Slezer says in his *Theatrum Scotiae* that three princes of Orkney and nine barons of Rosslyn are buried here. Since Sir William St Clair, the founder of the Chapel, was the third and last Prince of Orkney, both his father and grandfather must be buried here, the latter – unless he was reburied – at least thirty years before the Chapel was begun.

Opposite page. The Apprentice Pillar

Below. The story of Isaac, with the ram at top left

Bottom. Dragons at the base of the Apprentice Pillar

The room is rectangular and some thirty-six feet long. The engrailed cross of the St Clair family is carved on the roof. Along the south wall to the right of the altar you will find an aumbry (a small recess in the wall), a piscina to hold the holy water, and, to the right of the door, a fireplace.

On the right of the sacristy altar is a corbel with the coat of arms of the founder and that of his first wife, Lady Margaret Douglas, who died in 1452. On the left of the altar is a corbel with the St Clair engrailed cross. The colouring on both is modern.

It seems likely that the sacristy was used for services and perhaps also as a workshop during the forty years in which the upper Chapel was under construction. There are working drawings scratched on the walls, probably those of the craftsmen engaged in building the Chapel above.

With these exceptions, the sacristy is entirely bare of ornament, utterly unlike the upper Chapel.

The stained glass window of the transfiguration is the work of Patrick Pollen and was added in 1954 in memory of James Francis Harry, 5th Earl of Rosslyn.

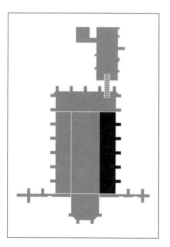

THE SOUTH AISLE

A S YOU CLIMB the stairs and return to the main Chapel, pause at the top and look at the window to your left. You will see a carving on each side, to the left a figure holding a cup and to the right an angel holding a scroll. Look above these figures and on the arch over the window you will see a carving of Indian corn or maize. In Chapter Five you can read about the significance which some observers attach to this (see page 54). Elsewhere in the building, on the architraves of the south aisle for example, you will see carvings of fern, curly kale, oak leaves, flowers, and other features of a local landscape familiar to the medieval masons by whose hand these images were crafted.

Stand now with your back to this window of Indian corn, facing north. On the architrave which joins the top of the Apprentice Pillar to the pillar on your left, in the left-hand corner, is a figure playing the bagpipes and immediately underneath the unlikely juxtaposition of a man asleep – although not all such instruments were as loud and martial as the highland bagpipes with which we are most familiar today.

In the right-hand corner, where Apprentice Pillar and architrave meet, you will see a figure of a crowned king, believed to be King Darius. On the architrave which joins the Apprentice Pillar to the south wall, running above the stairs to the sacristy, is an inscription in Lombardic letters. It reads: *Forte est vinu. Fortior est rex. Fortiores sunt mulieres: sup om vincit veritas,* meaning 'Wine is strong. The king is stronger. Women are stronger still: but truth conquers all.' (1 Esdras 3: 10–12) They are the three lines written

Window arch with carvings of Indian corn

as a trial of wisdom by the youths who formed King Darius' bodyguard and placed under the king's pillow while he slept. On awaking, the king invited the three young men to justify their words. Zerubbabel's observations about women and truth were adjudged the wisest and as a reward he was granted permission by the king to lead the Jews back to Jerusalem, in order to undertake the rebuilding of the temple.

Turn around with your back to the inscription and face down the aisle. On the architrave above you are a series of carvings on individual stone sections. On this side you will see the seven virtues. Starting from the left, we have first, as an introduction, a cardinal bishop with a crozier in one hand and a bible in the other. Then, from left to right:

1. Helping the needy
2. Clothing the naked
3. Looking after the sick
4. Visiting those in prison (if you look closely you will see the face of the prisoner at the barred window)

King Darius' trial of wisdom

The seven virtues (*top*) and the seven deadly sins (*above*)

5. Avarice (misplaced from the seven deadly sins) – a man with bags of money clasped to his chest

6. Feeding the hungry

7. Burying the dead

Then the reward for virtue, St Peter waiting at the gates of heaven with a key in his hand.

Walk along the aisle, turn around, and on the opposite side of the same architrave you will see the seven deadly sins. Starting from the left, there is a bishop with a staff in his hand as the introduction, then from left to right:

1. Pride – a Pharisee with puffed out chest

2. Gluttony – a man with a pitcher to his mouth

3. Charity (misplaced from the seven virtues)

4. Anger – a man with an axe in his right hand and a club in his left

5. Envy – a man with his hands across his chest surrounded by bunches of grapes

6. Sloth – a man with a bag dragging on the ground

7. Lust – the sinful lovers

And finally the punishment for sin, the devil emerging from a monster's mouth, symbolising hell, and stretching out a triple hook towards the whole group.

The most likely explanation for the reversal of Avarice and Charity is that when the stones of the architrave were carved in the workshop, the two scenes were carved on the wrong sides of their common stone. The geometry of the stone was such that it could not be included in the architrave the right way round, so the mason built it the wrong way and hoped no one would notice.

The conventional representation in Britain of the seven deadly sins is in the form of a tree or wheel, and their representation here in the form of a procession is exceptional, although there are many examples in France. As such, it is likely to have been the inspiration for the celebrated poem, 'Dance of the Sevin Deidly Synnis', which was written by the Scottish poet William Dunbar in about 1491, shortly after the death of the Chapel's founder.

Now look at the window to your right. At the bottom of the window, in the left hand-corner, is an angel holding a heart, said to be that of Robert Bruce (see page 42 in Chapter Four). In the right-hand corner is the figure of Moses, with horned head and the ten commandments. 'And when Moses came down from Mount Sinai, he held two tablets of the testimony, and he knew not that his face was horned from the conversation of the Lord.' (Exodus 34: 29.)

That Moses acquired horns is due to a mistranslation, since the Hebrew word *qeren* can mean either horn or ray of light. It seems more probable that Moses' face was decorated by the latter upon his return from Mount Sinai.

Turn to your right and continue walking westward along the south aisle until you reach the south door on your left. Above the wall pillar to the left of the door you may be able to make out a small carving of the veil of Veronica or Mandylion. St Veronica is holding up a veil on which is the image of Christ's head.

The legend is that as Jesus left the temple a woman handed him a veil on which to wipe his brow. When he returned the veil, his features were visible on the piece of cloth. The name Veronica is believed to derive from the Latin *vera*, meaning 'true', and the Greek *eikon*, meaning 'image'. A piece of cloth, said to be the original, is in St Peter's in Rome.

On the wall pillar to the right of the door you will see at the very top a carving which represents the presentation of the infant saviour in the temple.

Look at the window to your right. In the bottom left-hand corner of the window is a knight on horseback armed with a spear and behind him a figure holding a cross. It has been suggested that these figures may represent the legend of William 'the Seemly' St Clair, who is said to have carried back a portion of the true cross or 'holy rood' to Scotland. It is after this relic that Holyrood Abbey and Palace in Edinburgh are named.

Alternatively, the passenger may be Queen Margaret and the knight Bartholomew Ladislaus, a companion of William St Clair on that journey. It was Margaret's husband, King Malcolm Canmore, who encouraged the St Clairs to settle in Scotland.

Now walk into the choir and stop a few yards from the entrance to the baptistery, facing towards the organ loft. Here

Below. Angel holding the heart of Robert Bruce

Bottom. Knight on horseback

The apprentice (*left*), the mother of the apprentice (*centre*), and the master mason (*right*)

you will see the carvings of those involved in the story of the Apprentice Pillar. In the corner to your left, just below the empty statue niche, is the head of the apprentice with a scar on his right temple. To the left of the apprentice, at the same level, is the head of his grieving mother. To the right of the apprentice, in the other corner, is the head of the master mason.

Directly below the apprentice's head, at the top of the wall pillar, is the figure of William St Clair, the founder of the Chapel, holding a sword in his right hand. To the left are cockle shells, an emblem associated with St James. Together with the stars in the roof above they may symbolise the pilgrim's route to Santiago de Compostella (literally 'St James of the field of stars') in Spain.

Now we can leave the Chapel by the baptistery.

THE BAPTISTERY

William St Clair, founder of the Chapel

THE BAPTISTERY WAS added in 1880–1, together with the organ loft above. The organ itself had been built eight years earlier, in 1872, by the Edinburgh firm of David and Thomas Hamilton. It originally had two manuals without pedals and stood in the main Chapel. In 1882 it was moved to the new organ loft, and in 1902 was rebuilt and fitted with a pedal board.

There are two memorial windows in the baptistery. Both were commissioned by my father, the 6th Earl of Rosslyn, and are works of considerable merit. The window to your left is dedicated to my uncle, Pilot Officer The Hon. Peter St Clair Erskine, who died on active service in 1939, and to his stepfather, Wing Commander Sir John Milbanke, who died in 1947 from injuries also received during World War II. The stained glass is the design of William Wilson and was executed in 1950. The theme is an airman standing on the White Cliffs of Dover, with the St Clair and Milbanke family mottos – 'Fight' and 'Resolute and Firm' respectively – and the patron saints of Scotland and England, St Andrew and St George.

The opposite window is dedicated to my grandmother, Princess Dimitri, who died in 1969. The design and work are by Carrick Whalen and the window was completed in 1970. My grandmother was a great animal lover and the window's theme is St Francis of Assisi. He is surrounded by birds and butterflies, a squirrel, a rabbit, and, as a symbol of her Australian origins, a kangaroo.

Having left the Chapel through the baptistery, walk a few yards along the path towards the iron gates directly in front of you. If you turn and face the Chapel, you will see the unfinished east walls of the north transept to your left and the south transept to your right. These transepts would have formed the left and right arms of the cross, had the original, larger cruciform building been completed. Immediately to the left and right of the baptistery you can see the blocked-up openings which would have led to the north and south side aisles.

At the top right-hand corner of the blocked opening to your left is the figure of St Sebastian, who is being tied to a tree by two men and has been shot with arrows which hang from his left side (to the right as you look at him). At the top of the left-hand corner of the blocked opening to the right of the baptistery door is a carving of St Christopher carrying the infant Jesus.

Many of the external carvings are indistinct, but the extravagance of the building's stonework will become apparent as you explore the outside of the Chapel.

Above. Baptistery windows showing St Francis of Assisi (*left*) and an airman (*right*)

Below. The organ in the 1870s, before the building of the baptistery

CHAPTER III

CULTURAL HERITAGE

THE VILLAGE IS spelt Roslin, the Chapel, Castle, and earldom Rosslyn, but both derive from the Celtic words *ross*, a rocky promontory, and *lynn*, a waterfall. These are features of the scenery in the glen below, through which passes one of Scotland's most romantic rivers, the North Esk.

From its source high up in the Pentlands near the boundary between Midlothian and Peebleshire – now Tweeddale – it passes through Carlops, once a village of weavers, flows on through the gorge of Habbie's Howe and the woods surrounding Penicuik House, to Roslin Glen, Hawthornden, Melville Castle, and Dalkeith Palace, where it joins the South Esk and enters the Firth of Forth at Musselburgh.

Roslin Glen was settled by the Bronze Age and is the largest surviving tract of ancient woodland in Midlothian, in which over two hundred species of flowering plants and sixty species of breeding birds have been recorded. Several of the plant species are rare: the rough horsetail, wood-sedge, great horsetail, pendulous sedge, and wood melick. A mixed deciduous valley wood of oak, ash, and elm, the ground flora is characteristic of ancient woodland with continuous tree cover and contains wood-rush, wood sorrel, dog's mercury, ramsons, and opposite-leaved golden saxifrage.

From early in its history, Roslin Glen, with its castles of Rosslyn and Hawthornden, has been associated with historical and literary figures. The poet William Drummond, born in 1585 and said to be the first Scottish poet to write in pure English, lived at Hawthornden Castle, situated towards the north-east end of the glen. He was visited there in 1618 by Ben Jonson, Poet Laureate of England, who had made the journey from London to Edinburgh on foot. Drummond is said to have been sitting under a tree when his guest arrived and to have risen to greet him with the words,

'Welcome, welcome, royal Ben,'

to which, not to be outdone in courtesy or craft, Jonson replied,

'Thank ye, thank ye, Hawthornden.'

In the glen between Hawthornden and Rosslyn castles are several caves with large compartments, capable of hiding sixty or seventy men. The most famous is Wallace's Cave, so called because William Wallace is said to have taken refuge there during the Battle of Roslin in 1302. Sir Alexander Ramsay hid there from the English Army which captured Edinburgh in 1338, and Prince

Charles Edward Stuart, the Young Pretender, was sought but not found there in 1746.

Thomas Baynes, *Roslyn Chapel*. Lithograph, 1823

During the late eighteenth century, the notion that a place of natural beauty could be enhanced by its historical or literary past captured the imagination of writers and artists, and this led to Rosslyn's association with some of the most famous men of Scottish letters and inspired some of its greatest painters.

'Rosslyn and its adjacent scenery have associations dear to the antiquary and historian, which may fairly entitle it to precedence over every other Scottish scene of the same kind,' wrote Sir Walter Scott in his *Provincial Antiquities of Scotland* (1822).

It was to Lasswade, some three miles from Rosslyn, that Scott brought his bride, Charlotte Carpenter, in 1778:

Sweet are thy paths, oh passing sweet!
By Esk's fair streams that run,
O'er airy steep through copsewood deep,
Impervious to the sun.

His historical narrative, 'The Lay of the Last Minstrel', set in the mid sixteenth century and published in 1805, brought fame to Rosslyn with its mixture of architectural wonder, folklore, and history (see overleaf).

It was the contrasting glory of the past history of the St Clairs and the crumbling ruins of Rosslyn Castle which inspired eighteenth century poets such as Gillespie:

No more in Rosslyn's stately halls
The joyous feast is spread,
Mute rests the harp on Rosslyn's walls,
Its strings are damp and dead.

The spritely dance of prowest chiefs,
And tissued dames is o'er,
Yea all the pomp of feudal times,
In Rosslyn is no more.

and Byron:

Oh, Roslin! Time, war, flood and fire,
Have made your glories star by star expire.
Chaos of ruins! Who shall trace the void,
O'er the dim fragments, cast a lunar light,
And say 'Here was or is' where all is doubly night.

Alas! Thy lofty castle! And Alas!
Thy trebly hundred triumphs! And the day
When Sinclair made the dagger's edge surpass
The conqueror's sword in bearing fame away.

With its majestic landscape, waterfall, and ruined castle perched high on rocky promontory, Roslin Glen also provided the perfect symbol for the Romantic movement in landscape painting. This flourished in Scotland in the late eighteenth century under the Norie family, based in Edinburgh, to whom many of the great Scottish painters were at one time apprenticed.

They and their pupils found at Rosslyn a fusion of the classical influence of Claude's grand Italian landscapes with the picturesque charm of the wooded Scottish glen:

'Roslyn Castle . . . in its isolated and precipitous site – greatly enhanced by the romantic scenery of which it forms the centre – one of the most beautiful and picturesque ruins in Scotland.' (William Beattie, *Scotland*, vol. i, 1838.)

It rapidly became a landmark among Scottish landscape painters. Jacob More, 'the outstanding neo-classical painter' of his time and a pupil of Robert Norie, made some of his first sketches at Rosslyn, as recorded in 1797 by fellow artist John Beugo in his poem 'Esk Water':

The steepy banks that overhang thy wave
First rais'd the transport that his pencil gave.

Alexander Nasmyth, another pupil of Robert Norie, was also a frequent visitor to Rosslyn with his friend Robert Burns, the poet. Nasmyth recorded one of their visits in the late 1780's in a drawing of himself and Burns below the Castle. On another occasion, the two breakfasted together at the inn at Rosslyn after a

THE LAY OF THE LAST MINSTREL

O LISTEN, listen, ladies gay!
No haughty feat of arms I tell
Soft is the note, and sad the lay,
That mourns the lovely Rosabelle.

' – Moor, moor the barge, ye gallant crew!
And, gentle ladye, deighn to stay
Rest thee in Castle Ravensheuch,
Nor tempt the stormy firth today.

'The blackening wave is edged with white;
To inch and rock the sew-mews fly;
The fishers have heard the Water-Sprite,
Whose screams forbode that wreck is nigh.

'Last night the gifted seer did view
A wet shroud swathed round ladye gay;
Then stay thee, Fair, in Ravensheuch:
Why cross the gloomy firth today?'

' 'Tis not because Lord Lindesay's heir
Tonight at Roslin leads the ball
But that my Ladye-mother there
Sits lonely in her castle-hall.

' 'Tis not because the ring they ride,
And Lindesay at the ring rides well
But that my sire the wine will chide,
If 'tis not fill'd by Rosabelle.'

O'er Roslin all that dreary night
A wondrous blaze was seen to gleam;
'Twas broader than the watch-fire's light,
And redder than the bright moon-beam.

It glared on Roslin's castle rock,
It ruddied all the copse-wood glen,
'Twas seen from Dryden's groves of oak,
And seen from caverned Hawthornden.

Seem'd all on fire that chapel proud,
Where Roslin's chiefs uncoffin'd lie,
Each Baron, for a sable shroud,
Sheathed in his iron panoply.

Seem'd all on fire, within, around,
Deep sacristy and altar's pale,
Shone every pillar foliage-bound,
And glimmer'd all the dead men's mail.

Blazed battlement and pinnet high,
Blazed every rose-carved buttress fair –
So still they blaze, when fate is nigh
The lordly line of high St Clair.

There are twenty of Roslin's barons bold
Lie buried within that proud chapelle;
Each one the holy vault doth hold –
But the sea holds lovely Rosabelle!

And each St Clair was buried there
With candle, with book and with knell;
But the sea-caves rung, and the wild
    winds sung,
The dirge of lovely Rosabelle.

Sir Walter Scott, 1805

ramble in the Pentlands and were so delighted with the hospitality that they rewarded the landlady, Mrs Wilson, with two verses scratched on a pewter plate:

My blessings on you, sonsie wife!
I ne'er was here before;
You've gi'en us walth for horn and knife,
Nae heart could wish for more.

Heaven keep you free frae care and strife,
Til far ayont forescore;
And while I toddle on through life,
I'll ne'er gang by your door.

The inn is rich in literary association. Dr Johnson and Boswell took tea there on their way to Penicuik House following their tour to the Hebrides in 1773. William and Dorothy Wordsworth stayed there in 1803 and left early in the morning to visit Walter Scott at nearby Lasswade. They arrived to find him and his wife still in bed.

Like many of the old, rural church inns established for the accommodation of worshippers, the Rosslyn inn was situated next to the Chapel grounds. There the building stands today, now known as College Hill and no longer an inn.

The reputation of Rosslyn grew and by the turn of the eighteenth century many English painters included Rosslyn on their Scottish itinerary. Before Turner toured Scotland in 1801 his fellow artist Joseph Farington, who had visited Rosslyn in 1788, sent him directions to 'particular picturesque places'. Turner's sketches are housed at the Clore Gallery in London. There is a record of this and a subsequent visit Turner made to Rosslyn in 1818 in the engravings which illustrate Scott's *Provincial Antiquities of Scotland* (1822).

While the Romantic painters of the eighteenth century were drawn to the dramatic scenery of the North Esk and the ruins of Rosslyn Castle, it was the romance and mystery of the Chapel which captured the imagination of nineteenth century artists.

David Roberts, the painter who travelled extensively in Spain

Plaque outside College Hill, formerly the Rosslyn inn

THE OLD ROSSLYN INN (CIRCA 1660–1866)
HERE COUNTLESS TRAVELLERS TARRIED AWHILE AMONG THE DISTINGUISHED VISITORS WERE KING EDWARD VII WHEN PRINCE OF WALES DR SAMUEL JOHNSON AND JAMES BOSWELL ROBERT BURNS AND ALEXANDER NAYSMITH SIR WALTER SCOTT AND WILLIAM AND DOROTHY WORDSWORTH
ERECTED IN 1950 BY MRS HERBERTSON OF MELBOURNE AUSTRALIA DAUGHTER OF THE LATE CHARLES TAYLOR, CURATOR OF THE CHAPEL

Joseph Mallord William Turner R.A., *Roslin Castle*. Watercolour, circa 1820

and the Near East, was enchanted by the Chapel and painted several beautiful interior and exterior views in watercolour which date from the 1820's. So great was his enthusiasm for the building that he later became involved in a plan to restore the Chapel, along with other buildings of note in Edinburgh.

Samuel Dukinfield Swarbreck made a series of lithographs entitled *Sketches in Scotland* (1837–9), several of which take Rosslyn Chapel and Castle as their subject. The album bears a dedication to the 3rd Earl of Rosslyn. Engraved plates of Rosslyn Chapel appear in several nineteenth century architectural volumes, the minute detail of the Chapel interior lending itself to the precision of the engraver's art.

For William and Dorothy Wordsworth inspiration came from the unexpected beauty of the interior of the then neglected Chapel. Dorothy Wordsworth recorded their 1803 visit in her diary:

'The stone both of the roof and walls is sculptured with leaves and flowers, so delicately wrought that I could have admired them for hours. Some of those leaves and flowers were tinged perfectly green . . . and the natural product and the artificial were so intermingled that, at first, it was not easy to distinguish the living plant from the other, they being of an equally determined green.'

Her brother dealt with the same subject in his sonnet 'Composed in Rosslyn Chapel during a Storm', written in 1831:

The wind is now thy organist; a clank
(We know not whence) ministers for a bell
To mark some change of service. As the swell

David Roberts R.A., *The Interior of Rosslyn Chapel*. Watercolour, 1842

Of music reached its height, and even when sank
The notes in prelude, Rosslyn! to a blank
Of silence, how it thrilled thy sumptuous roof,
Pillars and arches – not in vain time-proof,
Though Christian rites be wanting! From what bank
Came those live herbs? By what hand were they sown
Where dew falls not, where raindrops seem unknown?
Yet in the temple they a friendly niche
Share with their sculptured fellows, that, green-grown,
Copy their beauty more and more, and preach,
Though mute, of all things blending into one.

It was presumably in this condition that Queen Victoria found the Chapel when she visited on September 14th, 1842. She is said to have been 'so much impressed with the beauty of the building, that she expressed a desire that so unique a gem should be preserved for the country.'

Rosslyn has remained a place of inspiration to all who visit. Walter Scott spoke of Harold, the 'bard of brave St Clair', who leaves behind scenes of war and turns to its peace and beauty:

With war and wonder all on flame,
To Rosslyn's bowers young Harold came,
Where, by sweet glen and greenwood tree,
He learned a milder Minstrelsy.

And of his own times there he wrote: 'It is a telling tale that has been repeated a thousand times to say that a morning of leisure can scarcely be anywhere more delightfully spent than in the woods of Rosslyn.'

I hope that you may find the time to walk a little in this beautiful landscape after your visit to the Chapel.

CHAPTER IV

THE ST CLAIRS OF ROSSLYN

THE ST CLAIR family are descendants of Rognvald 'the Mighty', Jarl or Chief of the Orkneys and Earl of Moere and Romsdahal in Norway, who was born in 835 AD. His son Rollo first fought and then in 912 made peace with King Charles 'the Simple' of France. At the treaty they signed at St Clair-sur-Epte, whence our family takes its name, Rollo was created 1st Duke of Normandy and he later married Gizele, one of Charles' daughters.

William St Clair subsequently came to England with his first cousin, William the Conqueror, and fought with him at the Battle of Hastings in 1066, as indeed did eight other St Clair knights.

In the years that followed many Anglo-Norman families, the St Clairs among them, came to Scotland. Some were disillusioned by King William's ruthlessness, others attracted by offers of land from King Malcolm Canmore, who had started to transform Scotland by reorganising its church and by introducing the feudal system. The latter depended on barons like St Clair. Father Hay, who made a study of the history of the St Clairs at the end of the seventeenth century, says that William St Clair soon became a favourite of King Malcolm and was nicknamed 'the Seemly St Clair' for 'his fair deportment'.

William escorted Malcolm's bride, the Saxon princess Margaret, from the court of Hungary, where she was brought up, to Scotland. He was made cup-bearer to Queen Margaret and obtained a life interest in the barony of Rosslyn. He was also made Warden of the Southern Marches with responsibility for defending Scotland's border area against the frequent attacks of the English, and on one of these expeditions he was killed.

He was succeeded by his son Henry, who was said to be 'of a free nature, and candid in his thoughts and words; very wise, and more given to study war than peace, for which rare qualities he was entrusted with military commands.' He was knighted by King Malcolm and awarded the barony of Pentland following a number of military successes against the English. He was with the king when Malcolm was killed in 1093 during the siege of Alnwick in Northumberland.

Henry's son, also Henry, was the first of the St Clairs to live at Rosslyn. Knighted by King David I and made a privy councillor, he was sent by King William the Lion as ambassador to Henry II of England, to reclaim from the English king the disputed territory of Northumberland. He fought at the Battle of Northallerton in 1138 and was rewarded with the gift of Cardain in 1153, thereafter

Coat of arms of the earls of Rosslyn

being known as Cardain Saintclair.

The barony of Rosslyn passed from father to son through several generations. Henry St Clair (succeeded 1243, died 1270) assisted King Alexander III in the capture of the Western Isles and William (1270–1297) was appointed ambassador to France. He was captured in the Battle of Dunbar in 1296 and died in the Tower of London in the following year.

Henry (1297–1331) and his two sons, John and William, fought at the Battle of Bannockburn. Robert Bruce rewarded Henry for his bravery with the gift of Pentland Moor. He was one of the Scottish nobles who in 1320 signed the Declaration of Arbroath, which proclaimed to the Pope Scottish independence from England. Henry's brother William was made Bishop of Dunkeld and displayed great valour in 1317 when he repelled an invasion of the English who had landed on the Fife coast while the king was in Ireland. Thereafter the king referred to William as 'the fighting Bishop'.

Henry's son William took part in the 'Royal Hunt' on the Pentland Hills. It is said that 'King Robert Bruce, in following the chase upon the Pentland Hills, had often started a white faunch deer, which his hounds were not able to catch. He asked his nobles around him if any of them had dogs swift enough to secure the prize. Of course none of them would like to affirm that his own hounds were superior to the King's, until Sir William was heard unceremoniously to exclaim that he would wager his head that his two favourite hounds, 'Help' and 'Hold', would kill the deer before she reached the march burn. The words being repeated to the King, he held him to his wager, and commanded all other hounds to be tied up, except a few ratches, or slow hounds, to start the deer. When the deer was started we are told that St Clair called upon Christ, the Blessed Virgin, and St Catherine for their help. As Sir William slipped his two favourite hounds, Douglas is said to have exclaimed

"Help, Hold, gin ye may

Or Rosslyn tynes his head this day."

The deer reached the middle of the burn when she was stopped by Hold and Help coming up, the deer was turned back and killed by Sir William's side.'

After the death of Bruce, this same Sir William was chosen along with Sir James Douglas and Sir Robert Logan of Restalrig to carry Bruce's heart to Jerusalem and deposit it in the Church of the Holy Sepulchre. They never reached their destination; during a fierce battle with the Moors at Teba in Spain in 1330 William, William's brother John, and Douglas were killed. The Moors were so impressed by the courage of the Scottish knights that they allowed the survivors to take their dead – and Bruce's heart – for burial back home.

Since William died before his father, Sir Henry was succeeded by his grandson, also William (1330–1358). He married Isabella de Strathearn, daughter of Malise, Earl of Caithness, Strathearn, and

Orkney. Malise had no male heirs and after William's death his and Isabella's son Henry was recognised as 42nd Earl of Orkney in 1369 and ten years later as the first St Clair Prince of Orkney. In addition to the titles inherited from his father, Henry also became Lord Shetland, Lord Sinclair, Lord Chief Justice of Scotland, Admiral of the Seas, Great Protector, and Keeper and Defender of the Prince of Scotland. His rank and influence were so great that he was allowed to issue coins within his own domains and to exercise judicial authority.

He was succeeded in 1400 by Henry, 2nd Prince of Orkney, described as 'a valiant Prince, well proportioned, of middle stature, broad bodied, fair in face, yellow haired, hasty and stern.' His marriage to Egida, daughter of Sir William Douglas, brought him the lordships of Nithsdale, the wardenship of the three marches, and six further baronies. 'He had,' Father Hay tells us, 'continually in his house 300 riding gentlemen and his Princess 55 gentlewomen whereof 35 were ladies. He had his dainties tasted before him. He had meeting him when he went to Orkney 300 men with red scarlet gowns and coats of black velvet.'

He was guardian to James I of Scotland during his minority. In 1406, the 12 year old prince was sent to the French court for education and safety and was accompanied by Sir Henry. There are two accounts of what happened during the voyage. One suggests that the young prince became seasick and the ship was forced to land on the English coast where all were taken prisoner by the soldiers of Henry IV of England. Alternatively, the prince and his escort sailed from North Berwick on a ship loaded with wool and hides but were captured off Flamborough Head, Yorkshire, by an English merchant vessel whose crew was rewarded by King Henry with the gift of the cargo.

The heir to the Scottish throne was taken to the Tower of London, where he remained in captivity for eighteen years. He was not allowed to return to Scotland until 1424, when he was 30, and then only in exchange for £40,000, a sum described as a bill for the upkeep and education of the young prince. Sir Henry obtained his own freedom in 1407 by payment of a ransom, although Hay has an alternative story:

'One John Johnstone of Pentland and tenant of Sir Henry went to England where his master was, and then played the fool so cunningly that without suspicion he gained entrance to the prison and one evening conveyed his master without the gate in disguised apparel. They travelled by night and rested by day; they found great enquiry for them when they came to the Borders. Two Southerns made for them and laid hold of their horses, but Sir Henry knew how to use his fists and struck one of them to the ground where he died. The other fled with shrieks and lamentable cries. Arriving in Scotland Sir Henry asked his deliverer what reward he would like but he declared that he wished no reward but that he might go to Pentland before he went to Rosslyn and pass three times around the linstone [boundary stone] which he duly did.'

J. Gellatly, *Rosslyn Church,*
ante 1700. Engraving

This is a good story and a pity to spoil it, but I hope that, if
true, my ancestor did rather more for him than John Johnstone so
modestly requested.

Sir Henry was succeeded in 1420 by William, 3rd Prince of
Orkney, described as 'a very fair man of great stature, broad
bodied, yellow haired, well proportioned, humble, courteous and
given to policy as building of castles, palaces and churches'. This
Sir William was the founder of the Chapel and also made
substantial additions to Rosslyn Castle.

He married first Margaret Douglas, daughter of Archibald, 4th
Earl of Douglas and 1st Duke of Touraine, and widow of the Earl
of Buchan. By this marriage he had one son, William, and four
daughters. Margaret died in 1452 and he married secondly
Marjory, daughter of Alexander Sutherland of Dunbeath, by whom
he had five sons, Oliver, William, David, Robert, and John.

The founder of the Chapel held vast territories and influence.
His power was seen by James III as a threat, the more so since Sir
William's sister was married to the king's brother, the Duke of
Albany. Relationships between king and brother were difficult and
at one stage James imprisoned Albany in Edinburgh Castle.

In 1455 James II had given Sir William the earldom of Caithness
in exchange for that of Nithsdale and in 1471 he received Ravenscraig
for the earldom of Orkney. James III had acquired Orkney by his
marriage to Queen Margaret of Denmark, and it was formally
annexed to the Scottish Crown by Act of Parliament in 1471.

During his lifetime Sir William divided his estates between his
three eldest sons: William, from his first marriage, and Oliver and
William, from his second. By far the best portions of the estate

J. Gellatly, *Rosslyn Castle, ante 1700*. Engraving

went to Oliver and thus his eldest son, known as 'William the Waster', was effectively disinherited. He received from his father only the barony of Newburgh in Aberdeenshire. Rosslyn, Pentland, and the more prestigious land went to Oliver. William the Waster disputed his brother's claim to Rosslyn and a subsequent contract between them was agreed, which confirmed Oliver's right to the estates at Rosslyn. But Oliver ceded to William other lands in Midlothian, together with the castles of Ravensheugh and Dysart in Fife. William was also afterwards declared by Act of Parliament chief of the St Clairs with the title of Baron Sinclair.

To the second son of his second marriage, also called William, Sir William had given in 1476 the earldom of Caithness. This 2nd Earl of Caithness fell at Flodden in 1513. It is the tomb of his grandson, the 4th Earl of Caithness, which you can see in the Chapel (see page 14).

Thus by the time of the founder's death in 1484, his vast possessions had been divided among three branches of his family: the Lords St Clair of Dysart, the St Clairs of Rosslyn, and the Sinclairs of Caithness.

The barony of Rosslyn passed to his son Oliver. A great favourite of the queen, he married a daughter of Lord Borthwick. He had four sons, George, Oliver, William, and John, the last becoming Bishop of Brechin and Lord President of the Court of Session and performing the marriage ceremony between Mary Queen of Scots and Henry Stuart, Lord Darnley, at Holyrood on July 29th, 1565.

Oliver was succeeded by his third son, William, who further endowed the Chapel. Thereafter the succession passed to William's eldest son, also William, who was made Lord Chief Justice of Scotland by Queen Mary in 1559, and in turn to his eldest son, Edward, who, having no children, made the estate over to his brother William.

This William also made significant additions to the Castle, building the vaults, the great hall and clocktower, and also the great turnpike of Rosslyn – the large stone staircase, four feet wide, leading up from the basement to the top floor of the Castle.

To his son William were granted the charters of 1630 from the Masons of Scotland, recognising that the position of Grand Master Mason of Scotland had been hereditary in the St Clair family since it was granted by James II in 1441. The original charters had been destroyed in a fire. He continued his father's work to the Castle, building over the vaults up to the level of the courtyard. It is his initials SWS with the date 1622 which can be seen above the door to the Castle today. He died on September 3rd, 1650, the day of the Battle of Dunbar.

His son John, called 'the Prince', held out for a time when the Castle was besieged in 1650 by Cromwell's troops under General Monk. Rare literary and historical treasures were destroyed in the bombardment from Monk's four pieces of ordnance and the assault of six hundred troopers. All that escaped the catastrophe were the sections still standing today. The east and west sides were battered down and the Castle sacked. John was captured and sent to Tynemouth Castle, only returning to Rosslyn shortly before his death in 1690.

His brother James was next in the line of descent. He was stepfather to Father Hay and was described by him as 'a very civil and discreat man'. He had two sons. The eldest, James, was killed at the Battle of the Boyne, leaving his brother Alexander to succeed. He was followed by his son William, the last male heir of the Rosslyn branch of the St Clairs.

This Sir William was considered by Sir Walter Scott, who knew him well, to be a Scottish laird of the old school and he described him thus:

'The last Rosslyn was a man considerably over six feet, with dark grey locks, erect and graceful, broad shouldered, athletic, for the business of war or chase, a noble eye of chastened pride and undoubted authority, and features handsome and striking in their general effect though somewhat harsh and exaggerated when considered in detail. His complexion was dark and grizzled and we schoolboys who crowded to see him perform feats of strength and skill in the old Scottish games of Golf and Archery, used to think and say amongst ourselves, the whole figure resembled the famous founder of the Douglas race. In all the manly sports which require strength and dexterity, Rosslyn was unrivalled, but his particular delight was in Archery.'

He was four times captain of the Honourable Company of Edinburgh Golfers and on three occasions, the last at the age of 68, won the Silver Club, which from 1744 was awarded in open

Sinclair clan badge

Sir George Chalmers, *Sir William St Clair of Rosslyn.* Oil, 1771

competition by the town of Edinburgh. He was also a brigadier of the Royal Company of Archers, the Queen's Body Guard for Scotland.

Having no male heir, he resigned his office as hereditary Grand Master Mason of Scotland to the Scottish Lodges at their foundation in 1736. The Lodges then appointed him as the first non-hereditary Grand Master Mason of Scotland at their meeting on St Andrew's day of the same year. Ironically, Sir William wasn't already a freemason, so he first had to be initiated into the Canongate-Kilwinning Lodge, whose chapel contains a full length portrait of him.

In his funeral oration in 1778 it was said that,

'Descended from an illustrious house, whose heroes have often bled in their country's cause, he inherited their intrepid spirit, united with the milder virtues of humanity and the polished manners of a gentleman . . . *non sibi sed societati vixit* [he did not

After James Northcote R.A., *Alexander Wedderburn St Clair, first Earl of Rosslyn*, by F. Bartolozzi. Engraving, 1800

live for himself but for his community].'

He had married Cordelia, daughter of Sir George Wishart, baronet of Clifton Hall, by whom he had had three sons and five daughters. But all died young except his daughter Sarah, through whom the succession then passed.

She married Sir Peter Wedderburn of Chester Hall and they had a son, Alexander, and a daughter, Janet. Janet was married to Sir Henry Erskine, 5th Baronet of Alva.

Alexander Wedderburn St Clair did much towards the preservation of the Chapel. He was also, in turn, Member of Parliament for the constituencies of Ayr Burghs, Richmond, Castle Rising, and Oakhampton. He became Solicitor General in 1771, Attorney General in 1778, Lord Chief Justice in 1780, and Lord Chancellor in Pitt's government of 1793, a post he held until 1801.

Friend of Adam Smith and David Hume, whom he defended in a case brought by the Kirk of Scotland, Wedderburn was a tough and ambitious individual with something of a temper. Having won a case in the Scottish courts before Lord Craigie, he was reprimanded for intemperate remarks he had made during the trial. He tore off his gown in a fury and vowed never to appear in a Scottish Court again; nor did he, considering that in any event the opportunities for advancement in Scotland were insufficient for a man of his ambition.

In 1780, he was created Baron Loughborough of Loughborough in the county of Surrey. Although twice married, he had no children and in 1795 he was created anew Baron Loughborough of Loughborough, this time in the county of Leicester and with provision for the title to be passed to his nephew. In 1801 he was created 1st Earl of Rosslyn in the county of Midlothian, with a similar provision for the succession. Records show that his disbursements in executing all of this amounted to £427.14.0.

When he died in 1805, he was buried in St Paul's Cathedral. He was succeeded by his nephew, Sir James St Clair Erskine, who was at various times Member of Parliament for Castle Rising, Morpeth, and Kirkcaldy, Director General of Chancery in Scotland, Lord President of the Council, and Grand Master Mason of Scotland. He married Henrietta Bouverie, daughter of the Hon. Edward Bouverie. When he died in 1837, he was succeeded by his son James Alexander St Clair Erskine, who became 3rd Earl of Rosslyn.

The 3rd Earl was Master of the Buckhounds and Under-Secretary of State for War in 1859. He married Frances Wemyss, daughter of Lt. General William Wemyss of Wemyss Castle in Fife. It was he who restored the Chapel as described in Chapter One. He died in 1866 and his second son, Francis Robert St Clair Erskine, became 4th Earl of Rosslyn.

Together with the title, he inherited from his father an estate in Fife of more than three thousand acres, worth over nine thousand pounds in rents and coal-mining royalties. He was High Commissioner to the General Assembly of the Church of Scotland on four occasions and captain of the Corps of Gentlemen at Arms. In 1870 he held a Grand Masonic Fette at Rosslyn attended by over one thousand freemasons and in the following year he was elected sixty-ninth Grand Master Mason of Scotland. When he indicated in the summer of 1871 that he did not wish to be considered for re-election, a petition of seven thousand signatures raised by the Lodges persuaded him to reconsider.

He married in 1866 Blanche Adeliza, second daughter of Henry Fitzroy and widow of the Hon. Charles Maynard.

The 4th Earl was a poet of some substance and there is reason to believe the tradition that he would have been made Poet Laureate in succession to Tennyson but for his death in 1890. He was the author of a volume of sonnets (1883) and *Sonnets and Poems* (1889), which included a Jubilee Lyric entitled 'Love that lasts Forever'. Written in 1887, it was dedicated to Queen Victoria and published at her command.

He was Ambassador Extraordinary to Madrid on the occasion of the marriage of Alfonso XII to Mercedes de Bourbon in January 1878, and when Alfonso's eighteen year old bride died in June of the same year, he wrote an elegy in her memory. In a letter from Madrid he recorded:

'The poor King remains leaning on her bed and calling her

Below. Hunting Sinclair tartan

Bottom. Masonic regalia of the 4th Earl of Rosslyn

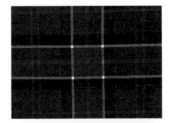

Top. The 4th Earl of Rosslyn, from *Vanity Fair*, November 12th, 1881

Middle. The 5th Earl of Rosslyn in Cuba, 1930, and his horse Buccaneer (*above*)

name Mercedes mia, Mercedes mia. To the last her eyes were turned on the King. I have seen him twice and all he said was that for him there was no consolation but that he would do his duty.'

He was a breeder and trainer of horses, and a member of the Jockey Club. One day a stud groom told him that a newborn foal had died in the care of a groom who had had too much to drink. 'Drunk?' queried the horrified Earl. 'Yes my Lord, drunk as a Lord, my Lord,' stammered the stud groom. 'Drunk as a bloody groom, you mean,' the Earl shot back.

He was buried at his own request in the south-west corner of the Chapel gardens, the first of a long line of St Clairs of Rosslyn to be buried outside the Chapel. A handsome monument to his memory and that of his wife, who died at the age of 94, can be seen there. It was carved in red sandstone by W. Birnie Rhind in 1899. In a letter to the 4th Earl's widow dated April 23rd, 1891, the estate architects remarked that Rhind seemed determined 'to obtain the order to do the work by estimating almost regardless, as it seems to us, of his own interests'.

The memorial is inscribed with a passage from one of the 4th Earl's sonnets:

Safe, safe at last from doubt, from storm, from strife,
Moored in the depths of Christ's unfathomed grave
With spirits of just, with dear ones lost,
And found again, this strange ineffable life,
Is life eternal: death has here no place, and
We enter life, but through the gates of death.

He was succeeded in 1890 by his eldest son, James Francis Harry St Clair Erskine, 5th Earl of Rosslyn, who married in the same year Violet, daughter of Robert Charles de Grey Vyner. At their wedding the Prince of Wales, later Edward VII, proposed the health of bride and groom. Harry was a close friend of the prince, who later became godfather to his son. Like the 4th Earl, he was a keen racehorse owner. A particular favourite was Buccaneer, who won the Gold Cup at Ascot. But he was also a gambler, and on one occasion bet £15,000 on Buccaneer to win the Manchester Cup. The horse lost.

He gambled at the roulette tables of Cannes and Monte Carlo and recounted his exploits in his autobiography, *My Gamble With Life* (1928). His gambling addiction cost him dearly. Six years after inheriting title, properties, estates, collieries at Dysart, assets of £50,000, and a steam yacht of great splendour, he had lost everything and was declared bankrupt.

The family silver, gold, and silver gilt plate was sold at a three-day auction in Edinburgh. A local paper reported that 'dealers were present from all over the kingdom and the continent'. Star of the sale was the magnificent Ascot Cup of 1892, designed and executed by Garrard, which was knocked down for £438.

On being made bankrupt he resigned his commission in the

Fife Light Horse, and he was rebuffed when he attempted to rejoin the regiment at the outbreak of the Boer War. Anxious to travel to South Africa, he secured a job as war correspondent for the *Daily Mail*. In this capacity he witnessed more of the campaign than he might have foreseen, taking part in the relief of Ladysmith and being taken prisoner on two occasions. He wrote about these experiences in his book *Twice Captured*.

Harry's sister Millicent married the heir to the Duke of Sutherland. She was just 14 when she accompanied her elder step-sister to Dunrobin Castle for a fortnight's holiday. It was the latter who was thought of as a possible match for Cromartie, the future 4th Duke. But Millicent sat next to him at dinner and he was intrigued by her attribiution of a family portrait. Few romances begin with the phrase 'Is that a Romney?', but a proposal followed six months later and they married in St Paul's Knightsbridge on her seventeenth birthday, when he was thirty-two.

Harry's own marriage to Violet ended when he was discovered by his father-in-law to have presented a £2,000 turquoise tiara to a lady friend. Before his divorce, Harry had joined with some friends to establish 'Lord Rosslyn's Theatrical Performances'. He now drew on that experience and joined a touring company. 'Of course the Prince of Wales has been none too pleased at my taking up an actor's career,' he wrote, 'and if we ever met was quite cold to me.' In 1897, he toured with *Trelawny of the Wells* in Newcastle, Glasgow, Edinburgh, Liverpool, and Manchester.

It was during his acting career that he met and within a few days married his second wife, Georgeiana. She was an American actress. The marriage lasted two years, and in 1908 he married for a third time.

In 1917 he was reinstated as a director of the collieries at Dysart and he worked there until 1923, when they were leased to the Fife Coal Company. Even when no longer living at Dysart he visited regularly, and one old resident recalled:

'I remember when I was a boy helping my grandmother to sell fish. We were in Fitzroy Street when this tall gentleman, beautifully dressed, crossed the street and took her by the shoulders and greeted her like an old friend. He asked her how the boys were, my father and uncles Bill, John, Dave and Archie. I didn't know who he was, and when he left he shook her hand. Who was that, I asked her. The Earl of Rosslyn, she said, and held out her hand showing two golden sovereigns among the fish scales; and I never saw it done.'

Harry died in 1939 and was succeeded by his grandson, my father, Anthony Hugh Francis Harry St Clair Erskine, 6th Earl of Rosslyn. My father took great interest in the Chapel and during the early 1950's undertook work to conserve it, as described in Chapter One. He died in 1977.

The 6th Earl of Rosslyn in coronation robes, 1953

CHAPTER V

PERSPECTIVES

ALTHOUGH THE LIFE of Rosslyn Chapel can be accounted for in part with some clarity, there remains much about its history that is less certain but nonetheless intriguing. It is perhaps not surprising that a place in which the pagan and Christian traditions mix so freely, and often confusingly, should attract mystics as well as historians. Indeed, the esoterica associated with Rosslyn deserve a book in themselves.

In this hinterland between history and fable stands Henry, 1st Prince of Orkney, who is said by some to have discovered America nearly one hundred years before Christopher Columbus. The story is as follows.

In fourteenth century Venice lived three brothers, Carlo, Antonio, and Nicolo Zeno. Carlo successfully repelled a Genoese attack on the city in 1380 and became known as 'the Lion of Venice'. Nicolo, it is said, was sailing around the north coast of Scotland when he was caught in a storm and shipwrecked in the Faroes. Rescued by a local chieftain called Zichmi, he summoned his brother Antonio from Venice and they entered Zichmi's service as admirals of his fleet. In 1393, they led an expedition to Greenland and successfully mapped the island, but in the following year Nicolo died.

Antonio made another expedition in 1398, this time with Prince Henry. With a fleet of 12 vessels and some two hundred men, they left the Orkney Islands and sailed, via Shetland, first to Newfoundland, where an unsuccessful attempt was made to land, and then into the heartland of Nova Scotia. Five ships were lost during the voyage. On arrival in Nova Scotia, Prince Henry is said to have sent the fleet back to Orkney, while he and his shore party of carpenters, shipwrights, sailmakers, and soldiers wintered with the Micmac Indians.

From Prince Henry is believed to originate the Micmac legend about the man/god Glooscap, the great lord who came from the east in a ship, taught them to fish with nets, and is still spoken of today. Prince Henry set out to return to Orkney in the spring of 1399. He sailed in what the Micmac Indians described as 'an island with trees growing on it', but ran into bad weather and was forced south, landing in what is now Massachusetts.

The story of the voyage was published in 1558 by Antonio Zeno's great great great grandson, and is known as the 'Zeno Narrative and Map'. The author claimed that the account was based on letters and diaries he had seen as a boy in the family archives, the majority of which had since been destroyed.

Opposite page. Figure of a medieval knight chiselled out of rock at Westford, Massachusetts, believed by some to represent Sir James Gunn of Clyth, a companion of Sir Henry on his voyage to America

52 PERSPECTIVES

Carvings of Indian corn in
Rosslyn Chapel

By the end of the sixteenth century the whole account was in
doubt and the authenticity of the manuscript was questioned, in
part because the places mentioned could not be found in the North
Atlantic. In 1784, however, a chronicler and companion of
Captain Cook called Johann Forster published a book in which he
argued that Zichmi was an Italian corruption of the name Sinclair
and that of the places mentioned, Frislanda was the Orkneys,
Estotilanda was Newfoundland, and Drogio was North America.

The truth may be hard to determine, but there is some
circumstantial evidence to support the story. First, the carvings on
the arch over one of the windows in the Chapel have been
identified as Indian corn or maize, a plant unknown in Britain at
the time the Chapel was built. Is it possible that knowledge
brought home by Prince Henry passed to his grandson William
St Clair, the founder?

Secondly, it was recorded in the 'Zeno Narrative' that a
companion and cousin of Prince Henry, Sir James Gunn of Clyth,
fell ill and died shortly after the landing in Massachusetts.
Chiselled out of the rock at Prospect Hill in Westford,
Massachusetts, is a carving of a fourteenth century knight in
basinet, camail, and surcoat. The shield was identified by a former
Lord Lyon as being from the Gunn family, and the sword has been
described as being of the period 1375–1400.

Thirdly, a canon which was dredged in 1849 from the harbour
at Louisburg on Cape Breton Island, Nova Scotia, has been
identified by some experts as a Venetian naval gun from the late
fourteenth century.

Antonio Zeno, in a letter home to Venice, wrote of Prince
Henry: 'If ever there was a man who was worthy of immortal
memory, it is this man.' Perhaps that is an appropriate epitaph.

Much has also been written about the links between Rosslyn
and the Knights Templar, and some of the carvings with Templar
associations have been described in Chapter Two.

In 1118, just after the death of Baldwin I, first Christian King
of Jerusalem, his cousin and successor Baldwin II was approached
by nine French knights who volunteered to protect pilgrims
travelling to the Holy Land. Lodgings were provided on the site of
the former stables of King Solomon, beside the site of the ruined
temple, and in 1128 they formally adopted the name of 'The Order
of the Poor Soldiers of Christ and the Temple of Solomon'.

Pope Innocent II placed the Templars under no earthly
authority but his own and the order grew and prospered until,
within a hundred years, it was the most powerful in Europe.

Some have speculated that the Templars were the military arm
of a more shadowy order, the 'Prieuré de Sion', and that the
Prieuré's purpose was to locate the hidden treasure of the temple,
which had been concealed from the soldiers of the Roman emperor
Titus, and use it to promote the order's political and spiritual aims.
Others have asserted that the Templars' real purpose was to seek
out, at the site of the temple, relics and manuscripts associated

WILLIAM DE St. CLAIR
KNIGHT TEMPLAR

with the secret traditions of Judaism.

Whatever the truth of the matter, it is fair to say that their financial acumen soon posed a threat to the feudal structure of Europe in general and the power of individual kings in particular. Having established what amounted to the first effective system of international banking, the Templars had made loans to most of the kings, princes, and prelates of western Europe.

King Philip 'the Bel' of France was one of their most indebted creditors and on October 13th, 1307, in collusion with Pope Clement, he invited the leaders of the order to a banquet at which he had grand master Jacques de Molay and other Templars arrested. Charged with heresy and idolatry, De Molay confessed under torture and was imprisoned. Later he recanted his confession and was executed. The order was proscribed throughout most of Europe after 1309. Some fled and others joined the Hospitaliers or Teutonic Knights.

So what of the connection with Rosslyn?

In the first place, the Templar leader Hugues de Payen, who was grand master between 1118 and 1136, was married to a Katherine St Clair; and two members of the St Clair family were

Tomb in Rosslyn Chapel of William St Clair, who died in Spain in 1330 while attempting to escort the heart of Robert Bruce to the Holy Land (see pages 14 and 42)

Carvings in the Chapel associated with freemasonry

allegedly grand masters of the Prieuré de Sion in the thirteenth and fourteenth centuries.

Also, it is known that some Templars who fled the persecution at the beginning of the fourteenth century came to Scotland. The Pope had excommunicated Robert Bruce because the Scots would not recognise Edward II of England as their king. Scotland and Portugal were the only two countries of western Europe where the order was not proscribed.

Masonic regalia of the 4th Earl of Rosslyn

At the village of Temple, a few miles from Rosslyn, is a ruined church of the order and also Templar Wood, a plantation in the shape of the splayed Templar cross. And carvings in Rosslyn Chapel, including the five-pointed star, the dove in flight carrying an olive branch, the floriated cross, and the artichoke, are said to have Templar associations.

Some writers have suggested that the voyage of Prince Henry to the New World was organised by the Knights Templar to seek a new home where their ideas could flourish. Others see the Chapel's and the St Clair family's masonic connections as significant, since freemasonry is believed by some to have been an escape route for Templar knights fleeing persecution.

The masonic connection was at no time more important than during the Civil War. While all around, including Rosslyn Castle, was put to flame, the Chapel was spared. This is said to have been in deference to the wishes of Cromwell, who was himself a freemason.

It has also been suggested that the Mason's Pillar and the Apprentice Pillar represent the pillars of Boaz and Joachim, which stood at the inner porchway of Solomon's Temple in Jerusalem, and that Rosslyn Chapel itself is a reproduction of the temple. Parallels have been drawn between the story of the Apprentice Pillar and the murder of Hiram Abif, master mason at the building of the temple, who was struck down by a blow to the head like Rosslyn's apprentice.

Rosslyn Chapel has been proposed at various times as the repository for artefacts ranging from the lost Scrolls of the Temple to the true Stone of Destiny.

The legend that William 'the Seemly' St Clair retrieved a portion of the true cross has been described on page 31. Others ascribe significance to an extract from the 'Acts of the Lords of Council in Public Affairs, 1501–1544', which reads: 'The Lords ordain William Sinclair of Roslin to produce within three days all jewells, vestments and ornaments of the Abbey and places of Halyrudtous . . . put and ressavit within his place.' This refers to items supposedly taken to Rosslyn Chapel from Holyrood for safekeeping prior to an English attack in 1544. Some people believe these treasures remain hidden at the Chapel to this day.

All these claims, suppositions, and theories add to the Chapel's aura of intrigue and mystery and bring to Rosslyn a splendidly diverse range of visitors.